Order this book online at www.trafford.com
or email orders@trafford.com

Most Trafford titles are also available at major online book retailers.

Cover Design, Marc Little (www.marclittle.com)
Chapter Title Graphics, Gustave Doré & Marc Little

Printed in Victoria, BC, Canada.

ISBN: 978-1-4251-5967-2 (sc)
ISBN: 978-1-4251-5968-9 (e-book)

*We at Trafford believe that it is the responsibility of us all, as both individuals
and corporations, to make choices that are environmentally and socially sound.
You, in turn, are supporting this responsible conduct each time you purchase a
Trafford book, or make use of our publishing services. To find out how you are
helping, please visit www.trafford.com/responsiblepublishing.html*

*Our mission is to efficiently provide the world's finest, most comprehensive
book publishing service, enabling every author to experience success.
To find out how to publish your book, your way, and have it available
worldwide, visit us online at www.trafford.com*

Trafford rev. 04/13/2010

 www.trafford.com

North America & international
toll-free: 1 888 232 4444 (USA & Canada)
phone: 250 383 6864 ♦ fax: 812 355 4082 ♦ email: info@trafford.com

The Secret Joy
of repentance

By
Two Hermits

One who prayed   for one who wrote

To Professor Bruce M. Metzger
with esteem and gratitude

Contents

The Strength of Silence

I t is written in the lives of the desert fathers, that a young monk went to the wilderness of Scete to see Abba Macarius and ask him for a word of counsel. And the old solitary said to him: "Go back, remain in your cell, and your cell shall teach you everything."[1]

Silence is a great teacher, and the first thing we learn from her is our need for peace and quietness. Man is body and soul, and just as the body requires cessation of physical activity to reinvigorate itself, so does the soul need peace and silence for its own well-being and tranquillity.

Without rest, the body collapses, and if not allowed to repose in sleep, the mind becomes disordered and incapable of good judgment. Moreover, not only does the sleep-deprived mind lose its capacity to think well and make good decisions, but in enforced wakefulness, it can impose upon consciousness: a dream world. Without sleep, we shall hallucinate, and things will become so disorganized that we shall have an overwhelming desire to close our eyes and slumber off to escape the confusion. We had better get some sleep, then, or suffer a mental break-down.

In the beginning of His ministry, when the fame of His miracles had already spread His name abroad, "great multitudes came to hear, and be healed by Him" but Jesus "secretly withdrew Himself to the wilderness and prayed."[2] He left the crowds that sought Him.

He did the same thing again, this time by the shores of Lake Galilee: "when Jesus saw great multitudes around Him,

He commanded" His disciples to take Him by boat "to the other side"[3] of the lake away from the crowd. Why?

He did so to teach us a very important lesson: the need to prepare ourselves, to pray, to gather our thoughts and renew our strength before an important task. Not only before a work, but after its completion. This we learn from the episode: "when the apostles came together to Jesus and told Him all the things they had done and the things they had taught. And He said to them: 'Come you yourselves apart to a desert place, and rest awhile.' And so "they went away in the boat to a lonely place by themselves." St. Mark tells us that they did so 'because many were coming and going, and they had no leisure even to eat.'"[4] True, they needed to take time to feed their bodies at leisure, and to nourish their souls as well, because:

Man does not live by bread alone but by (the other "bread" also, of) every Word that proceeds from the mouth of God.[5]

We derive our physical well-being from food and rest. If the Word of God is the food of the soul, silence is the rest that also strengthens it.

Keep silence before me, O islands, and let the people renew their strength.[6]

In quietness and in trust shall be your strength.[7]

The prophetic cry to "hear the Word of the Lord!"[8] is also a call for us to be silent. The Word of God speaks only if we are silent. The better part that Mary chose and Martha[9] forgot is the attentive silence that sits by the Lord and draws Him to speak, because it is a silence that encloses the Word, and embraces it. What can the living Word desire more than to be longingly heard? Attentive silence draws forth the words of instruction from a teacher.

O Job, hear me; be silent and I will speak.[10]

Be silent and I will teach you wisdom.[11]

It is in silence that the Word of God shall resound in the depths of our being, and awaken us to a new life strengthened by the knowledge of the Lord. The knowledge we gain by partaking the bread of His Word in silence; the Word that is the food and strength of our souls.

Just as we receive strength and energy from eating ordinary "bread that strengthens the heart of man,"[12] so it is that we can receive "the power of understanding"[13] after we have understood the bread of His Word, which has now become for us: "the bread of understanding."[14]

There is strength in understanding, that is why in Holy Scripture these are often paired:

God... is mighty in strength and understanding.[15]

I am Understanding, I have strength.[16]

Thus, when it is said that "the Lord shall... feed His flock with strength,"[17] it is also meant that He shall strengthen them with knowledge and understanding:

I will give you shepherds after my own heart, who shall feed you with knowledge and understanding.[18]

To understand the Word of the Lord is to understand the truth, wisdom and knowledge within it, from which we receive strength for the soul:

Great is truth and stronger than all things... it endures and is always strong.[19]

We cannot do anything against the truth.[20]

Wisdom and knowledge shall be the stability of your times and the strength of salvation.[21]

Wisdom is better than strength... Wisdom is better than weapons of war.[22]

Wisdom strengthens the wise more than ten mighty men....[23]

A wise man is strong, yes, a man of knowledge increases strength.[24]

St. Peter, who was asked by the Lord to feed His lambs and His sheep,[25] was also told by Him to "strengthen your brothers"[26] :to fortify them in the knowledge of the Lord.

The greatest lesson that silence shall teach us is that we progress from understanding His Word to knowledge of the Lord Himself:

Make me to know Your ways that I may know You.[27]

Be filled with the knowledge of His will in all spiritual wisdom and understanding... increasing in the knowledge of God.[28]

That the God of our Lord Jesus Christ, the Father of glory, may give you the spirit of wisdom and revelation in the knowledge of Him.[29]

The ancients knew that we shall find Him in His Word:

His Image is the most holy Word.[30]

From my youth You have appeared to me in the understanding of Your judgments.[31]

It is when we shall have found Him in His Word that we shall find the Source of all our strengthening:

The Lord is the strength of my life.[32]

O God, the Lord, the strength of my salvation.[33]

He shall strengthen your heart.[34]

And so the first thing is to be silent - to listen to the gentle Voice[35] within. Then, at last, shall we be satisfied[36] with the vision of Him - the end of all knowing.

Be silent, and know that I am God.[37]

REFERENCES

1. "The Paradise of the Holy Fathers." Translated from the Syriac by E. A. Wallis Budge, London, 1907. Vol. II, P. 16
2. St. Luke 5:15-16
3. St. Matthew 8:18
4. St. Mark 6: 30-32
5. Deuteronomy 8:3; St. Matthew 4:4; St. Luke 4:4
6. Isaiah 41:1
7. Isaiah 30:15
8. Isaiah 1:10; Jeremiah 2:4
9. St. Luke 10:38-42
10. Job 33:31
11. Job 33:33
12. Psalm 104:15
13. 2 Esdras 4:22; Enoch 14:3
14. Sirach 15:3
15. Job 36:5
16. Proverbs 8:14
17. Micah 5:4
18. Jeremiah 3:15
19. I Esdras 4:35, 38
20. 2 Corinthians 13:8
21. Isaiah 33:6
22. Ecclesiastes 9:16, 18
23. Ecclesiastes 7:19
24. Proverbs 24:5, A.V.
25. St. John 21:15, 17
26. St. Luke 22:32
27. Exodus 33:13
28. Colossians 1:9, 10
29. Ephesians 1:17
30. Philo Judaeus (c. 20 B.C.-46 A.D.), "De Confusione Linguarum" 97
31. Hymn Scroll, IQH9:31, Dead Sea Scrolls
32. Psalm 27:1
33. Psalm 140:7
34. Psalm 27:14; 31:24
35. 1 Kings 19:12-13
36. Psalm 17:15
37. Psalm 46:10, literal translation

The Secret Joy of Repentance

We may be as silent as we can be, and ponder day after day in some remote corner, but we shall never understand the hidden wisdom and knowledge of His Word unless we are good - unless we repent.

Nothing worthwhile, nothing wonderful, nothing really moving will happen to us unless we repent, and take the blindfold off our eyes. Because, to repent is to be able to see things in a new light, and with a new understanding of it all. The very word for "**repentance**": *metanoia*, used in the Greek of the Gospels, is a composite of two words: *meta* meaning "*change*" and *noeo*, to "*understand.*"

True repentance produces so dramatic a transformation of our understanding that the Greek word gives the effect rather than the real meaning of repentance. On the other hand, the common Hebrew word for repentance: *shub* is more explicit since it signifies a "*turning back*" or "*returning*" to God.

But there is another word for "repentance" used in the Old Testament which also conveys the wonderful effects of it, and that is the Hebrew word *nacham* which means "*comforting.*" For the Lord readily comforts those who, sorrowing for their sins, return to Him.

The Lord does a very gracious thing for those who repent. He opens the doors of His treasury, and reveals to them: the precious things of His wisdom and knowledge. Thus the repentance of a sinner is not only a cause of joy for the angels in heaven [1], but also for the sinner himself who returns to the Lord.

Because, "whenever a man shall be converted to the Lord, the veil shall be taken away"[2] and he shall see and understand what was hidden from him:

> *True repentance of a godly sort destroys ignorance, and drives away the darkness, and enlightens the eyes, and gives knowledge to the soul, and leads the understanding to salvation. And those things it has not learnt from man, it knows through repentance*[3]

The repentant sinner is shown beautiful things he never understood before, in order to draw him to the benefits of right living. For pale in comparison are the vain allurements of the world which formerly enticed him.

"Let us therefore repent, and pass from ignorance to knowledge, and from foolishness to understanding."[4] For the early Fathers knew that "repentance is itself understanding."[5] Indeed, "to repent is great understanding."[6]

Not only did the early Christians know that but the Jews as well. Philo Judaeus wrote: "Repentance... means passing from ignorance to understanding... from senselessness to prudent insight,"[7] and in the Talmud we read: "the perfection of wisdom is repentance."[8] The Jews know that "repentance on earth leads to reception of the highest secrets in heaven."[9] But we do not have to take their word alone for it, they merely repeated what the Lord Himself promised through His servants, the prophets:

> *Repent, o backsliding children... and I will give you shepherds after my own heart who will feed you with knowledge and understanding.*[10]

> *Repent, and turn yourselves away from all your transgressions ... and get yourselves a new heart and a new spirit.*[11]

> *They will repent, acknowledging that I am the Lord their God and I shall give them a heart and ears that hear.*[12]

So, "let us return to the Lord... then we shall know."[13] And let us with Daniel the prophet "make our prayer before the Lord our God that we might turn away from our iniquities and understand His truth."[14] For, if we return to the Lord, Wisdom herself shall instruct us:

Repent at my reproof, and behold, I will pour My spirit to you, and I will make My words known to you.[15]

I was converted, I repented, and after that I was instructed.[16]

The Lord said: "They will return to Me with their whole heart... and I will give them a heart to know Me that I am the Lord."[17] Did not St. Paul write to Timothy to "be gentle to all men, apt to teach, patient, correcting opponents with gentleness so that God may perhaps give them repentance towards the full knowledge of the Truth"? [18] For, "God, our Savior, will have all men to be saved (through repentance), and come to the full knowledge of the Truth"[19] after they have repented.

How wonderful repentance is! Let us find out how we go about repenting. But first, let us know what repentance is *not*. Repentance is not penance. The word "penance" is derived from the Latin *poena* which means "punishment." In the spiritual sense penance is punishment voluntarily accepted in retribution for offenses. It does not necessarily imply a change in character or conduct.

Repentance is not remorse. The word "remorse" is derived from two Latin words, *re*: "to do again" and *mordere*: "to bite", such as the shaking of the head and grinding of one's teeth that follows the realization of having done something wrong or stupid. By itself, remorse has no redemptive value. Repentance is not self-condemnation for having sinned, because self-condemnation leads to self-hatred; and self-hatred to self-destruction - suicide.

What then is repentance? And how can we receive that marvelous transformation of our understanding promised by the very word repentance?

We shall have truly repented when we are sorry for our sins, and have completely turned away from all that leads us to sin, and have also turned towards the Lord.

> *Return to me with your whole heart, with fasting, and weeping and mourning; rend your hearts...*[20]

> *Let the wicked forsake his way, and the unrighteous man his thoughts; and let him return to the Lord for mercy; to our God who is generous in forgiving.*[21]

To repent is to reject totally that which turned us away from God, firmly determined never to offend Him again. For the Lord, who forgave and healed sinners, also said to them: "Go, and sin no more,"[22] Repentance is not static, but moves towards God with heroic resolve, leaving all sins behind. Repentance not only hates evil and departs from it but turns and does what is good, and learns to love and cleave to goodness:

> *Cease to do evil, learn to do good.*[23]

> *Abhor that which is evil and cleave to that which is good.*[24]

Repentance not only makes us mortify our corrupt inclinations but also impels us to develop the opposite virtues. Unless we have radically abandoned our former ways and are now endeavoring to do better, we have not really repented. Because, to repent means to change: to be converted to a new manner of living, and a life now pleasing to the Lord.

We are not going to repent unless we become aware of the sinfulness of sin, the "abominable thing"[25] that sin is before the eyes of God. For there is no repentance without a sense of guilt, a consciousness of not having lived and done as we should.

Thus, the **first** step towards repentance is **conviction**, the realization that there is something wrong in our way of living which must be set aright. This inward acknowledgment of our sinfulness and the need to be forgiven is a great gift from God.

It is the Holy Spirit "who shall convince the world of sin, and of righteousness, and of judgment."[26] Having convinced us of the reality of sin and of sinfulness He shall make us "know therefore that it is an evil thing and bitter, that we have forsaken the Lord our God and that His fear is not in us."[27] Conviction of the evil of sin is not a work of nature but of grace; not of man's own spirit but of the Spirit of God. He who shall convince us of sin shall also convince us of righteousness and make us desire to be good, and walk in the ways of the Lord:

Show me Your ways, O Lord; teach me Your paths.[28]

Show us the way that we should go and the thing that we should do.[29]

Lord... make me repent that I may repent.[30]

The **second** step we take towards repentance is **contrition**: the sincere regretting of all the wrongs we have done because they have not only offended our neighbor but the Lord Himself who loves us. True sorrow for sins brings forth tears as when "the Lord turned and looked upon Peter, who had denied Him three times, and Peter remembered the Word of the Lord... [31] and Peter went out and wept bitterly."[32]

When we gaze upon and see what He did for us, when we look upon Him whom we have pierced by our indifference, our hearts should rend in contrition. Then, shall we know that:

The Lord is near to the brokenhearted and saves those who are of a contrite spirit.[33]

For thus says the High and Exalted One who inhabits eternity, whose Name is Holy: 'I dwell in the high and holy place, also with him who is of a contrite and humble spirit, to revive the spirit of the humble, and to revive the spirit of the contrite.[34]

Godly sorrow leads to repentance...[35]

The **third** step, close to repentance, is **change**: changing our attitudes, changing our ways and changing our actions. The change towards good that comes when we become convinced that we have done wrong and are truly sorry. "For godly sorrow produces repentance that leads to salvation."[36] The salvation that comes when we have changed our ways for His way, our broad way "that leads to destruction"[37] for His "narrow way that leads to life."[38] Great is the change that repentance demands of us:

Unless you be converted and become as little children, you shall in no way enter the Kingdom of Heaven.[39]

For a grown-up person to become like a child again is a very great change indeed. Yet we must change that much to become truly converted. The truth is that we cannot do so by ourselves. But let us take heart, because St. Paul tells us that it is "the goodness of God which leads you to repentance."[40] God wills our repentance:

God... now commands all men everywhere to repent.[41]

Repent, for the Kingdom of Heaven is at hand.[42]

The Lord wills our repentance because He wants us to become perfect children of God: "Be ye perfect as your heavenly Father is perfect."[43] And He sent His disciples to preach "repentance and remission of sins... in His Name to all nations"[44] because He promised[45] that if we ask for anything in His name it will be granted to us, and we can have repentance welling forth from our hearts in the name of the Lord Jesus. For it is Jesus whom "God has exalted as Prince and Savior to give repentance and forgiveness of sin"[46] to us if we cry out to Him:

Lord... make me repent that I may repent.[47]

Lord, if You will, You can make me clean.[48]

And the Lord who is "moved with compassion"[49] will again say to us:

Return to Me, for I have redeemed you.[50]

I will. Be you made clean.[51]

Let repentance arouse in us indignation for our sins, the holy fear of the Lord, a hunger and thirst to be good,[52] a longing to be like Him, and a passionate desire to set ourselves right with God.

Let us know the agony that it is to be away from Him, the bitter anguish of having brought forth nothing for Him, of having worked for Him as a chore without love.

And let us beg Him from the dry ground of our hearts to come and plow, and sow and harrow, and rain upon it true repentance for our sins, so that we may someday bring forth from the ground He has sown:

Fruits worthy of repentance.[53]

REFERENCES

1. St. Luke. 15:7, 10
2. 2 Corinthians 3:16
3. Testament of Gad 5:7-8
4. Clement of Alexandria, *Exhortation*, Chapter 10
5. Shepherd of Hermas, *Mandates* IV. 30:2
6. Idem.
7. Philo Judaeus, De Virtutibus, 180
8. Babylonian Talmud, *Berakoth* 17a
9. *Midrash Talpiyot*, 166a by Rabbi Eliyahu ha Kohen, Warsaw, 1875. First Edit. Smyrna 1736.
10. Jeremiah 3:14, 15
11. Ezekiel 18:30, 31
12. Baruch 2:30-31
13. Hosea 6:1, 3
14. Daniel 9:13
15. Proverbs 1:23
16. Jeremiah 31:19
17. Jeremiah 24:7b, a
18. 2 Timothy 2:24-25
19. 1 Timothy 2:3, 4
20. Joel 2:12, 13
21. Isaiah 55:7
22. St. John 8:11; 5:14
23. Isaiah 1:16, 17
24. Romans 12:9
25. Jeremiah 44:4
26. St. John 16:8
27. Jeremiah 2:19
28. Psalm 25:4
29. Jeremiah 42:3
30. Jeremiah 31:18
31. St. Luke 22:61
32. St. Luke 22:62
33. Psalm 34:18
34. Isaiah 57:15
35. 2 Corinthians 7:10
36. Idem.
37. St. Matthew 7:13

38. St. Matthew 7:14
39. St. Matthew 18:3
40. Romans 2:4
41. Acts 17:30
42. St. Matthew 4:17
43. St. Matthew 5:48
44. St. Luke 24:47
45. St. John 14:13, 14; 16:23-24, 25-26
46. Acts 5:31
47. Jeremiah 31:18
48. St. Matthew 8:2; St. Mark 1:40
49. St. Matthew 9:36; 14:14; 18:27, etc.
50. Isaiah 44:22
51. St. Matthew 8:3; St. Mark 1:41
52. St. Matthew 5:6
53. St. Matthew 3:8

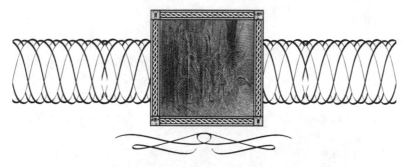

The Bread of Understanding

The Teaching of the Lord is perfect, converting the soul, the Testimony of the Lord is sure, making wise the simple.[1]

There is something about the beauty of Holy Scripture that touches the heart, and fills it with an inexpressible yearning towards good. A word here, a phrase there, and all at once a chord is struck and the soul awakens, irresistibly drawn by the Voice she once heard.

The grateful Psalmist promised the Lord: "I will teach transgressors Your ways, and sinners shall be converted to You,"[2] for "the Teaching of Truth... turns many away from iniquity."[3] When Wisdom cries out "and Understanding puts forth her voice"[4] sinners listen, awestruck by the sonorous ring of Truth. There is no force more capable of breaking the most hardened heart than the Word of God, which has also the power to enkindle it:

> *Is not My Word like a fire? Says the Lord, and like a hammer that breaks the rock in pieces?*[5]

When "the Word of God came to John the son of Zechariah in the wilderness," and he began "preaching the baptism of repentance for the remission for sins... the multitudes... came forth to be baptized by him."[6] Then "went out to him all the country of Judea, and all the people of Jerusalem, and they were baptized by him in the river Jordan, confessing their sins,"[7] because they were drawn to repentance by the power of the Word of God.

If we want to be touched by His Word and impelled to repent, we must "hear not only with the outward ear, but in the depths of the heart"[8] For it is possible to "have ears to hear but hear not,"[9] and to "hear... indeed and understand not"[10] if our hearts are closed. As the Lord said to those who rejected Him:

Why do you not understand My speech?
Because you cannot hear My word.[11]

Their pride made them "deaf in understanding."[12] In the time of Nehemiah, "all who could hear with understanding" were those who "were attentive" to His words. It was they who were moved and "wept when they heard the words of the Law,"[13] because His words have power to rouse up those who listen with their hearts. Let not His ministers forget the Lord's reproach to the priests of His people:

If they had stood in My counsel and had caused the
people to hear My words, then they would have turned
them from their evil ways and from the evil of their doings.[14]

And let His people remember the wonderful prayer Solomon made to the Lord:

Give Your servant a heart that hears (shamea) ...
that I may understand.[15]

Only if we listen to His Words with open hearts shall we be moved to repent and thereby understand, for to repent is to depart from evil, and "to depart from evil is understanding."[16] They who understand strive to keep His commandments because they have experienced the great joy that it is to understand His Word:

There is no joy above the joy of the heart.[17]

Your Word was unto me the joy and rejoicing of my heart.[18]

The Lord gives understanding to those who repent so that Understanding may guard them and deter them from sin:

Understanding shall watch over you.[19]

Understanding... shall preserve you.[20]

If a man understands the design of God by which all things are ordered he will despise all material things, and his vices will be healed.[21]

The temperate understanding has power to conquer the pressure of the passions.[22]

That is why the Psalmist cried out to the Lord:

Give me understanding and I shall keep Your Law, yes, I shall observe it with all my heart.[23]

I will run the way of Your Commandments when You shall enlarge my understanding.[24]

The Essenes thanked the Lord for the help they received from understanding in their struggle to remain faithful to the Law of the Lord:

I thank You, O Lord, for You have put understanding in the heart of Your servant, that he may do what is good and right before You and restrain himself against deeds of wickedness.[25]

You have taught him understanding of Your mysteries that he may not sin against You.[26]

And they shared with others who desired to be righteous, the understanding that made them cleave to the good:

He shall instruct them in the marvelous and true Mysteries... that they may walk with one another in perfection in all that has been revealed to them.[27]

They knew the power towards good that understanding exerts on those who have gone astray:

Teaching understanding to those whose spirit has gone astray, instructing in doctrine those who murmur.[28]

The men of old knew that understanding helps us to be good:

I have understanding through the abundance of Your goodness .... I have bound myself not to sin against You and not to do anything of all that is evil in Your eyes.[29]

Give to Your people a heart of wisdom and an understanding of prudence, and ... they shall not sin.[30]

If men saw, not with bodily eyes but with the eyes of the understanding they would certainly be converted to virtue.[31]

But we do not have to search out ancient writings when we can find the same Truth expressed in our own Bibles:

The secret things belong to the Lord our God; but those things which are revealed belong to us and to our children forever, so that we may do all the words of this Law.[32]

They who are understanding... turn many to righteousness.[33]

He shall turn the hearts... of the disobedient to the under-standing of the just.[34]

And who shall know Your thought unless You give wisdom and send Your Holy Spirit from above so that the ways of men may be corrected, and men may learn the things that please You?[35]

He opens the understanding of men... to turn a man from unrighteousness.[36]

The Lord give you insight and understanding... that you may keep the law of the Lord your God.[37]

And if "the Sons of men having no understanding of these things, sin and provoke the Most High,"[38] whose fault is it?

My Tabernacle is spoiled and all My cords are broken, My children have departed from Me and they are gone... because the shepherds have become brutish and have not sought the Lord therefore they shall not understand, all their flocks shall be scattered.[39]

They are shepherds who cannot understand.[40]

But we must not lose heart for "Jesus... was moved with compassion towards them, for they were as sheep without a shepherd and so He began to teach them many things."[41] And the Lord promised that:

I will give you shepherds after My own heart who will feed you with knowledge and understanding.[42]

If therefore you also have a good understanding then will both the wicked man be at peace with you and the profligate will reverence you and turn unto good.[43]

What is it about Understanding that gives it such a hold on the human heart and allures it towards good?

It is because we have been created with a deep hunger in our hearts for the Wisdom and Knowledge of God. The repentant heart is given to eat "the bread of understanding,"[44] so that it may no longer be famished but know that in the Word of the Lord it has at last joyfully found its nourishment and strength.

Thus, when our Lord gives us wisdom, understanding, and knowledge, He feeds them to us. And He invites us not only to "desire the sincere milk of His word,"[45] but to long for "the bread of understanding," and "the water of wisdom to drink."[46]

Did not Wisdom cry out: "Come, eat of my bread and drink of the wine I have mingled"?[47]

The Lord said in Isaiah: "Come... why do you spend your money for that which is not bread, and your labor for that which does not satisfy? Hear Me with attention, and eat what is good, and delight yourselves in fatness. Incline your ear, and come to Me, hear, and your soul shall live"[48] - fed by His Word.

And so, in the wonderful wisdom of God, when the Lord Himself came to us, He "stood and cried out saying:

If anyone thirst, let him come to Me and drink.[49]

And let him eat for He also said:

I am the Living Bread which came down from heaven; if anyone eats of this bread, he will live forever.[50]

And he shall rejoice in the Living Bread - the joy of our desiring; that "Bread of Life":[51]

In whom are hid all the treasures of wisdom and knowledge.[52]

REFERENCES

1. Psalm 19:7
2. Psalm 51:13
3. Malachi 2:6
4. Proverbs 8:1
5. Jeremiah 23:29
6. St. Luke 3:2, 3, 7
7. St. Mark 1:5
8. Testament of Isaac, 1:6
9. Jeremiah 5:21
10. Isaiah 6:9
11. St. John 8:43
12. Clement of Alexandria, *Exhortation X*
13. Nehemiah 8:2, 3, 9
14. Jeremiah 23:22
15. 1 Kings 3:9
16. Job 28:28
17. Sirach 30:16
18. Jeremiah 15:16
19. Proverbs 2:11
20. Proverbs 4:5, 6
21. Corpus Hermeticum, *Asclepius* III.22
22. 4 Maccabees 3:17
23. Psalm 119:34
24. Psalm 119:32
25. 1 Q H 14:8, 9 - Dead Sea Scrolls
26. 1 Q H 17:22 - Dead Sea Scrolls
27. I Q S 9:18, 19 - Dead Sea Scrolls
28. 1 Q S 10:26-11:1 - Dead Sea Scrolls
29. 1 Q H 14:17, 18 - Dead Sea Scrolls
30. Ps. Philos, *Biblical Antiquities* XXI. 2
31. Philo, *Questions on Genesis* IV. 51
32. Deuteronomy 29:29
33. Daniel 12:3
34. St. Luke 1:17, literal translation
35. Wisdom 9:17-18 - Latin Vulgate Text
36. Job 33:16, 17 Greek Text
37. 1 Chronicles 22:12
38. Testament of Levi 3:10

39. Jeremiah 10:20-21
40. Isaiah 56:11
41. St. Mark 6:30, 34
42. Jeremiah 3:15
43. Testament of Benjamin 5:1, literal translation
44. Sirach 15:3
45. 1 Peter 2:2
46. Sirach 15:3
47. Proverbs 9:5
48. Isaiah 55:1, 2, 3
49. St. John 7:37
50. St. John 6:51
51. St. John 6:48
52. Colossians 2:3

Watching

The understanding that the Lord gives us after we have repented, is a great gift from God which we should cherish and keep, for it is given to encourage and help us remain in the ways of the Lord. Along with this insight into the wonderful hidden wisdom found in His Word, is a grave responsibility, because "the greater the knowledge given to us, the greater the risk we incur."[1] "For if we sin deliberately after receiving the knowledge of Truth, there no longer remains a sacrifice for sins, but a fearful prospect of judgment, and a fury of fire which will consume..."[2] "When a righteous man turns away from his righteousness and commits iniquity and does the same abominable things that the wicked man does, shall he live?... he shall die"[3] says the Lord.

All who return to wickedness after having departed from evil "shall be tormented, because having understanding they yet wrought iniquity"[4] "He who transgressed even though he understood, yes, for this very reason he shall be tormented."[5] For "a man shall utterly perish who having had the knowledge of the way of righteousness forces himself into the way of darkness"[6] again. "For if, after they have escaped the defilements of the world through the knowledge of our Lord and Savior Jesus Christ, they are again entangled in them and overpowered, the last state has become worse for them than the first. For it would have been better for them never to have known the way of righteousness than after knowing it to turn back from the holy commandment delivered to them,"[7]

"Better is a man who has less wisdom, and wants

understanding with the fear of God, than he who abounds in
understanding, and transgresses the Law of the Most High."[8]
For the Lord's "anger comes upon... one who turns back from
righteousness to sin, the Lord shall prepare him for the sword,"[9]
because it is written that "a man who departs from the way of
understanding shall remain in the congregation of the dead."[10]
For "if he goes astray (after "Wisdom reveals to him her secrets
v. 18), Wisdom will forsake him and cast him off,"[11] inasmuch as
Wisdom said:

> "I... will reveal to him my secrets, but if he turns away from
> me I will forsake him and deliver him to the destroyers."[12]

"One who has come to know God (through repentance)
ought not to do evil, but do good" for "the ones who have known
God... and do evil will be doubly punished and will die forever."[13]
We know that "when a man shall be converted to the Lord
the veil shall be taken away"[14] and he shall see the hidden
things of the Word "having been enlightened in the eyes" of
his "understanding."[15] But along with that insight comes the
imperative to persevere in the right path. "For it is impossible
to restore again to repentance those who have once been
enlightened, who have tasted the heavenly gift, and have become
partakers of the Holy Spirit, and have tasted the goodness of the
word of God, and the powers of the age to come, if they then
commit apostasy,"[16] denying the Lord and returning to their
former ways.

Understanding shall indeed "watch over"[17] us and
"preserve"[18] us, but we must also keep watch over our secret
inclinations, and watch out that we do not forsake the ways of
the Lord. For "that servant who knew the Lord's will and did
not prepare himself nor did according to His will, he shall be
beaten with many lashes";[19] "to him who knows how to do good
and does it not, to him it is a sin."[20] When we are given greater
perception into the Mysteries of God, we must use that increase
of vision not only to enjoy the beautiful things of the Lord, but to

watch for the given signs[21] of His Coming, and watch over others
and ourselves.

The first thing Understanding shall teach us is the
importance of watching, because we first learn by seeing before
we get to understand what is heard. Even in prayer, awareness
of the One to whom we pray should precede our prayer to Him.
Seeing the need motivates the action. Thus we are told to "watch
and pray"[22]; or as St. Peter said: "Be... sober, and watchful that
you may pray."[23]

They who see the hidden wisdom and knowledge of His
words long to behold the wise and knowing Author. Therefore,
the first thing we are exhorted to watch for are the signs of the
Coming of the Lord. And because we are told to be ready for it,
the Gospels also ask us to prepare ourselves, to "watch... for you
know not the day nor the hour when the Son of Man shall come"
[24]; "watch... lest He come suddenly and find you asleep. And
what I say to you I say to all: Watch."[25]

How do we prepare ourselves by watching? By realizing that
our secret self has a secret inclination towards evil:

Watch yourselves very well... lest you corrupt yourselves.[26]

Watch yourselves that you be not snared.[27]

*Watch... lest there be in anyone of you an evil unbelieving heart
leading you to fall away from the living God.*[28]

Being mindful of that propensity towards sin, we are
counselled to be alert at the very origin of all watching:

Watch yourself that you do not look at evil.[29]

Watch over a shameless eye.[30]

We should also watch what we hear and how we hear, for
what we take in can influence us towards good or evil, and in

proportion to our attention to His words we shall be given to understand:

Watch that no man deceive you.[31]

Watch and beware of the leaven (evil counsel) of the Pharisees and the leaven (unscrupulousness) of Herod.[32]

Watch how you hear.[33]

Most of all we must watch what we say by watching over our tongue, for as St. James tells us: "the tongue no man can tame" it is "a restless evil, full of deadly poison."[34] Our Lord warned us: "Let what you say be simply 'yes' or 'no', anything more than this comes from the evil one.[35]

It is not an easy thing to watch over our mouth: "Who shall set a watch over my mouth?"[36] We may need the help of Almighty God there, because extra effort is required:

Set a guard, O Lord, before my mouth, keep the door of my lips.[37]

I will guard my ways that I may not sin with my tongue; I will muzzle my mouth.[38]

Truly, we must guard or watch over our ways, and we do that by keeping watch over our own particular weaknesses and evil inclinations.

Are we prone to acquisitiveness?

Watch and beware of all covetousness; for a man's life does not consist in the abundance of his possessions.[39]

Do we have a tendency to be proud and crave adulation?

Watch that you do not despise one of these little ones.[40]

Watch out of practicing your piety before men in order to be seen by them.[41]

Just when we seem to be doing all right, let us watch out that we do not become overconfident:

Let everyone who thinks that he stands watch lest he fall.[42]

And let us watch out for infidelity:

Watch your spirit that you do not deal treacherously.[43]

Watch that you fulfill the ministry which you have received in the Lord.[44]

What else should we watch? We should watch that we do not forget His Words:

Watch yourselves, and watch over your souls diligently, lest you forget what your eyes have seen and lest they depart from your heart.[45]

Watch yourselves, lest you forget the Covenant of the Lord your God.[46]

Let us remember that "man does not live by bread alone"[47] but by that other "Bread" also, from which he receives the strength and help that his soul needs:

How can a young man keep his way pure?
By keeping watch over Your Word.[48]

Your word I have hid in my heart that
I may not sin against You.[49]

Let us not forget to "watch and pray" that we enter not into temptation,"[50] for there is someone we must watch out for, who seeks to ravage our souls:

Be sober, be vigilant, because your adversary the devil prowls around like a roaring lion, seeking someone to devour. [51]

"Watch and pray" for "the Lord knows how to deliver the godly from temptation," [52] and He does not forsake those who keep their eyes on Him:

My eyes are ever towards the Lord for He shall pluck my
feet out of the snare.[53]

And because the Lord commanded us to "love one another"[54] as He loved us, we should watch over each other because one who loves, cares for, and is solicitous over the wants of others. That is the kind of "watching" the Good Samaritan[55] did, who felt compassion for the wounded man and provided for his needs.

Who does not remember the story of the Prodigal Son: "While he was still a great way off, his father saw him and had compassion, and ran and fell on his neck and kissed him."[56] For that loving father was watching with yearning for his lost beloved son.

Above all we should keep watch in our hearts over that most important thing upon which all watching depends:

Watch yourselves well that you love the Lord your God.[57]

Let us watch ourselves well, and see to it that we love as we should, Him Who loves and watches over us with such infinite care:

You shall love the Lord your God with all your heart and
with all your soul, and with all your strength.[58]

REFERENCES

1. 1 Clement 41:4
2. Hebrews 10:26, 27
3. Ezekiel 18:24
4. 2 Esdras 7:72 (Codex Sangermanensis)
5. 2 Baruch 15:6
6. Epistle of Barnabas 5:4
7. 2 Peter 2:20-21
8. Sirach 19:21, Latin Vulgate Text
9. Sirach 26:28, Greek Text
10. Proverbs 21:16
11. Sirach 4:18-19, Greek text
12. Sirach 4:18-19, Hebrew Text
13. Shepherd of Hermas, *Similitude* IX 95:1,2
14. 2 Corinthians 3:16
15. Ephesians 1:18
16. Hebrews 6:4-6
17. Proverbs 2:11
18. Proverbs 4:5, 6
19. St. Luke 12:47
20. St. James 4:17
21. St. Matthew 24:3-41; St. Mark 13:4-30; St. Luke 17:20-37; 1 Thess 5:2-3
22. St. Matthew 26:41; St. Mark 14:38
23. 1 Peter 4:7
24. St. Matthew 25:13; 24:42; St. Mark 13:33, 35
25. St. Mark 13:35, 36-37
26. Deuteronomy 4:15-16
27. Deuteronomy 12:30
28. Hebrews 3:12
29. Job 36:21
30. Sirach 26:11
31. St. Matthew 24:4; St. Mark 13:5
32. St. Mark 8:15; St. Matthew 16:6, 11
33. St. Mark 4:24
34. St. James 3:8
35. Sr. Matthew 5:37
36. Sirach 22:27
37. Psalm 141:3
38. Psalm 39:1

39. St. Luke 12:15
40. St. Matthew 18:10
41. St. Matthew 6:1
42. 1 Corinthians 10:12
43. Malachi 2:16
44. Colossians 4:17
45. Deuteronomy 4:9
46. Deuteronomy 4:23
47. St. Matthew 4:4; St. Luke 4:4
48. Psalm 119:9
49. Psalm 119:11
50. St. Matthew 26:41; St. Mark 14:38
51. 1 Peter 5:8
52. 2 Peter 2:9
53. Psalm 25:15
54. St. John 15:12, 17
55. St. Luke 10:25-37
56. St. Luke 15:20
57. Joshua 23:11
58. Deuteronomy 6:5

Seeking God

When we love someone with all our heart and soul, we seek the one we love. We seek to embrace whom we love with all our heart's desire.

To repent is not only to have sorrow for sin and turn away from evil but to turn towards the Lord as well - to humbly seek the One whom we have offended and make our peace with Him.

God, who commands us to love Him, is not an abstract definition, a concept or a force, but a person: "the living God."[1]

God is a Discovery and we are on this earth to discover Him. He is "the God of Abraham, the God of Isaac, and the God of Jacob,"[2] because each one of them discovered Him, and to each one God revealed Himself in a special and personal way. So that each one of them could say of Him what doubting Thomas exclaimed in awe and reverence:

My Lord and my God! [3]

The Lord then is Someone who is to be discovered by us. Someone we should search for and who is always ready to transform our lives the moment we shall encounter Him.

God hides:

Truly You are a God who hides Himself,
O God of Israel, the Savior.[4]

I will wait upon the Lord who hides His face from
the house of Jacob, and I will look for Him.[5]

God hides so that we may go and seek Him, and keep on looking for Him until we find Him whom our heart and soul desire.

Our life on this earth should be a continual search, a seeking for God so that we may find Him, and having found Him, keep Him ever by our side. For to find God is to keep Him, if we really love Him:

> *When I found Him whom my soul loves, I held Him, and would not let Him go...*[6]

Throughout Holy Scripture we are exhorted to seek the Lord:

> *Seek ye My face.*[7]

> *Seek the Lord and His strength, seek His face continually.*[8]

And we are given the assurance that:

> *If you seek Him, He will be found by you.*[9]

And lest we should become discouraged by a long and seemingly fruitless search, we are also told how to go about seeking the Lord in order to find Him:

> *You shall find Him, if you seek Him with all your heart and with all your soul.*[10]

We shall find Him if we seek Him with the same intensity of desire with which we are told to love Him. Bring desire into your search for Him and you will most assuredly find Him:

> *I will seek Him whom my soul loves.*[11]

> *They entered into a covenant to seek the Lord, the God of their fathers, with all their heart and with all their soul... they... sought Him with their whole desire and He was found by them.*[12]

Seek the Lord with all desire and longing:

As a deer longs for water, so does my soul long for You, O God, my soul thirsts for God, for the living God. Oh, when shall I come and behold the face of God?[13]

My soul yearns for You in the night, my spirit within me earnestly seeks You early at dawn.[14]

God wants to be sought for with all longing by us:

I remember you, the devotion of your youth, the love you had for Me as a bride, how you went after Me in the wilderness, in a land that was not sown.[15]

But where are we to find God? In our search we may feel like Job who cried out:

Oh, that I knew where to find Him![16]

Let us not forget that first of all we must repent and prepare ourselves before we can seek God and find Him:

Everyone... prepared his heart to seek God.[17]

He set himself to seek the Lord.[18]

Set your heart, and your soul to seek the Lord your God.[19]

How do we prepare our heart and soul to seek God? We prepare, the day we are determined to keep His Commandments, the day we take stock of ourselves and repent, thereby receiving understanding and having our eyes opened to be able to see Him whom we hope to find. For unless we become clean of heart we shall not be able to see and discover Him:

Blessed are the pure in heart, for they shall see God.[20]

To discover the Lord is to want others to share the joy of finding Him. Thus, we are told that St. John the Baptist saw Him and got St. James and St. John to follow Him. And St. Andrew saw Him and got his brother St. Peter, and brought him to the Lord. And when "Jesus... found Philip and said to him: 'Follow Me,'" Philip found Nathaniel and said to him: 'We have found Him of whom Moses and the Law and also the Prophets wrote: Jesus of Nazareth... come and see.' [21] All they who love God want others to love Him too.

Before we set off to seek and find Him, we have to take stock of ourselves and take a good look at the chamber of our heart to see who is there, what is there taking up the place that rightfully belongs to Him. In other words we have to "clean house" and clean up the room we shall bring Him into. For to find the Lord is to hold on to Him, and bring Him inside us so that He may abide in our hearts. For the Lord desires to come and live with us:

Behold, I stand at the door and knock, if anyone hears My voice and opens the door, I will come in to him...[22]

Abide in Me and I in you.[23]

He is the Bridegroom of our soul, the Beloved we should yearn to love: "when I found Him whom my soul loves, I held Him, and would not let Him go until I brought Him into my house and into the chamber of"[24] - my heart. When we shall find Him and bring Him into our heart, let us make sure there is no one else within who should not be there, because the Lord is a jealous God and He will not tolerate any rivals:

I the Lord your God am a jealous God.[25]

The Lord whose name is Jealous is a jealous God.[26]

My glory I will not give to another, neither My praise.[27]

You cannot serve God and Mammon.[28]

As a jealous Lover the Lord remonstrates against the faithless soul, using the same words an aggrieved husband does before a perfidious wife. And He takes the same steps to win back the soul as a man does to gain back his errant spouse:

She went after her lovers, and forgot Me, says the Lord.
Therefore, behold, I will allure her to the wilderness and I will
speak to her heart... and in that day says the Lord,
you will call Me, 'My Man.'[29]

We owe Him our love and fidelity, because our souls are meant to be married to the Lord:

Return, O backsliding children, says the Lord, for I am married
to you.[30]

Your Maker is your husband.[31]

And it is in our fidelity to the Lord that we shall know Him, in that intimate kind of knowing in which a spouse knows her husband and is known by him:

I will espouse you to me in faithfulness; and you shall know the
Lord.[32]

What has happened to that kind of love between God and man? St. Paul prophesied that in the last days:

There will come times of stress... Men will become lovers of self,
lovers of money... lovers of pleasure rather than Lovers of God.[33]

Have we become lovers of someone else, of something else? Or are we truly "lovers of God"? We had better love the Lord with all the human Love we have in our hearts or we shall be considered unworthy by Him and cast aside. Such is the ardor of His love, and the love He desires from us, that He becomes intolerant of anyone else, even our most cherished ones, should they attempt to come between our love for Him and His love for us:

*If anyone comes to Me and does not hate his own father
and mother and wife and children and brothers and sisters,
yes, and even his own life, he cannot be My disciple.*[34]

*He that loves his father or mother more than Me
is not worthy of Me.*[35]

We owe Him all our human love, for He gave Himself up completely out of His great love for each and every one of us. woe to us if we do not respond wholeheartedly to the immensity of His love for us:

If anyone love not the Lord Jesus Christ, let him be accursed.[36]

How are we to know if we really love the Lord? The answer to that is to ask ourselves: are we seeking Him? Are we anxious to return to Him, to tell Him of our love for Him and hear Him tell us of His love for us?

God is always asking us that eternal question:

Do you love Me?[37]

And when He looks down from heaven at us, Does He not look to see if we are seeking Him?:

*The Lord looks down from heaven upon the children of men to
see if there is anyone who understands and seeks God.*[38]

If we are not seeking Him as we should, it is because there is a dimension missing in our repentance: the realization of what it entailed Him in pain and suffering to ransom us from the penalty of our sins. Only when we have experienced the need to be forgiven shall we be truly sorry and turn to the Lord, who is always ready to forgive us. And only then shall we seek and follow after Him with all the love of our hearts, because one to whom much has been forgiven loves much in return.

Have we not yet returned to Him? Have we not yet sought the Lord? Let us afflict ourselves. For thus says the Lord:

Turn to Me with all your heart, and with fasting, and with weeping, and with mourning, rend your heart and not your garments and turn to the Lord your God.[39]

In their affliction they shall seek Me early.[40]

And we shall find Him waiting for us with open arms:

For the Lord our God is gracious and merciful and He will not turn away His face from you if you return to Him.[41]

REFERENCES

1. Psalm 42:2
2. Exodus 3:6; St. Matthew 22:32; St. Mark 12:26
3. St. John 20:28
4. Isaiah 45:15
5. Isaiah 8:17
6. Song of Songs 3:4
7. Psalm 27:8
8. 1 Chronicles 16:11
9. 1 Chronicles 28:9
10. Deuteronomy 4:29
11. Song of Songs 3:2
12. 2 Chronicles 15:12, 15
13. Psalm 42:1-2
14. Isaiah 26:9
15. Jeremiah 2:2
16. Job 23:3
17. 2 Chronicles 30:18, 19; *Idem.* 19:3; Ezra 7:10
18. 2 Chronicles 20:3
19. 1 Chronicles 22:19
20. St. Matthew 5:8
21. St. John 1:29, 35-37, 40-42, 43, 45, 46
22. Revelation 3:20
23. St. John 15:4
24. Song of Songs 3:4
25. Exodus 20:5
26. Exodus 34:14
27. Isaiah 42:8
28. St. Matthew 6:24; St. Luke 16:13
29. Hosea 2:15, 16, 18 Literal Translation
30. Jeremiah 3:14
31. Isaiah 54:5
32. Hosea 2:20
33. 2 Timothy 3:1, 2, 4
34. St. Luke 14:26
35. St. Matthew 10:37
36. 1 Corinthians 16:22
37. St. John 21:15, 16, 17
38. Psalm14:2; 53:2

39. Joel 2:12, 13
40. Hosea 5:15 AV
41. 2 Chronicles 30:9

The Vision of Faith

In willingly taking up our daily tasks, and in "bearing one another's burdens,"[1] and in giving up our wants to fill the needs of others, we make the preparation most acceptable before the Lord. We amend our lives by denying ourselves for the love of others in the same way the Lord atoned for our sins:

> *By this we know love, that He laid down His life for us; so ought we to lay down our lives for the brethren.*[2]

Repentance breaks down the hardened heart; compassion softens it. We need to exercise both in order to prepare our hearts to seek the Lord. Repentance shall give us the understanding we need to seek: "the heart of him who has understanding seeks,"[3] just as the Lord "searches out the deep and the heart, for He has good understanding,"[4] but we also have to be merciful and kind towards others to receive the light we need to find Him whom we are seeking:

> *Is not this the fast that I choose: to loose the bonds of wickedness, to undo the heavy burdens to let the oppressed go free, and to break every yoke? Is it not to share your bread with the hungry, and bring the homeless poor into your house; when you see the naked, to cover him, and not to hide yourself from your own flesh? Then shall your light break forth like the dawn… If you draw out your soul to the hungry, and satisfy the afflicted soul, then shall your light rise in the darkness…*[5]

"God made... the heart for understanding"[6] and so we "understand with the heart,"[7] but only if our hearts are not hardened:

Do you not yet perceive or understand, are your hearts hardened?[8]

They did not understand about the loaves because their heart was hardened.[9]

They are darkened in their understanding... due to their hardness of heart.[10]

Man not only understands with the heart but man "believes with his heart"[11] also, if his heart is not hardened:

He upbraided them for their unbelief and hardness of heart.[12]

Some were hardened and did not believe.[13]

The wicked have neither faith nor understanding in their hearts:

An evil and unbelieving heart.[14]

Evil men do not understand.[15]

And since it is with the heart that we believe and understand, the call to repentance is also an invitation to believe:

Repent and believe in the Gospel.[16]

Repentance towards God, and faith towards our Lord Jesus Christ.[17]

Thus, there is a close relationship between faith and understanding:

That you may... believe and understand that I am He.[18]

You have given Your understanding, O Lord, to Your believers.[19]

Keep My faith... and understand My Knowledge.[20]

Conversely:

If you do not believe neither will you at all understand.[21]

They believe not God nor understand His Power.[22]

For if the heart is hardened to belief, it is also hardened to understanding and there is great darkness in the soul:

The god of this world has blinded the understanding of the unbelievers to keep them from seeing the light of the Gospel.[23]

Repentance not only gives us the joy of understanding but the light of faith as well, so that we may have "the clear vision which faith affords"[24] in our search for the Lord. The pure in heart shall see God, but it is with the eyes of faith that we shall discover the signs of His presence. We shall see Him in the end of our search if we are good: "I will behold Your face in righteousness,"[25] but we must first "repent and believe"[16] before we eventually come to know Him:

We believe and have come to know that You are the Christ, the Son of the Living God.[26]

I know (now) whom I had believed (before).[27]

Before we can seek God with all our heart and soul we must first have faith in Him, "for whoever would draw near to God must first believe that He is"[28] - that He exists. Faith gives us "the assurance of things hoped for, the conviction of things not seen"[29] as yet with the outward eye, but nevertheless believed in, because they have been discerned by the inward vision of faith.

"Faith... is the gift of God"**30** given to those who have
repented, the moment they have resolved to be faithful to Him
and have commenced to do good.

Fidelity not only gives us understanding: "a good understanding have all those that do His Commandments,"**31** but faith as
well. Abraham was a man of faith, for "Abraham believed God,"**32**
but it was not his faith that was praised by the Lord, but his
righteousness which gave him the gift of faith:

*Abraham believed the Lord; and He reckoned it to him as
righteousness.***33**

*It shall be our righteousness if we observe to do all these
Commandments before the Lord our God as He commanded us.***34**

When we "depart from evil and do good"**35** towards the
unfortunate, we are also rewarded by the gift of faith which we
receive in helping them, for "has not God chosen those who
are poor in the world to be rich in faith?"**36** If you "out of your
abundance supply their need," you may be sure that the poor
"out of their abundance shall supply your need"**37** - Faith.

Someday, if we remain faithful to Him, "we shall see Him as
He is,"**38** and behold Him "face to face,"**39** but in the meantime
we need the vision of faith to discover the secret signs of His
presence that lead us to Him. "Believe in Him and He will help
you"**40** to find Him, because He will teach you where to look:

*Teach me good understanding and knowledge, for I have
believed...***41**

*It is to men of faith that the heavenly secrets are revealed.***42**

*You... reveal what is hidden to the pure who in faith have
submitted themselves to You and Your Law.***43**

"Has anyone ever trusted in the Lord and been confounded?"**44**

No, because "they who put their trust in Him shall understand Truth."[45]

The first truth we shall understand from Him in our search is that His hand is clearly manifest in the things that He has made:

Lift up your eyes on high and see: who created these?[46]

The heavens declare the glory of God, and the firmament shows His handiwork.[47]

Ever since the creation of the world His invisible nature, namely, His eternal power and deity, has been clearly perceived in the things that have been made.[48]

For by the greatness of the beauty of creation, and of the creature, the Creator of them may be seen so as to be known thereby.[49]

With the eyes of faith we shall see His hand not only in creation but in ourselves:

I will praise You, for I am awesomely and wonderfully made; marvelous are Your works, and that my soul knows right well.[50]

And we shall also see the hand of God in our lives and in the course of events around us. The Holy Scriptures "bear witness"[51] to Him but we need faith and understanding to see and hear the witness of the Word:

By faith we understand...[52]

A man of understanding, understands the Word.[53]

I gave them the words which You gave Me, and they have accepted them and they have truly known that I came forth from You.[54]

There are no stumbling blocks for those who believe and understand, because "faith" can "remove mountains,"[55] and "His hand levels the way for those who believe in Him."[56]

They who believe keep on seeking Him unmindful of any obstacles, because they know that "they who seek the Lord shall understand all things."[57] And they rejoice in searching for Him with hope in their hearts, knowing full well that:

The Lord... shows Himself to those who have faith in Him.[58]

REFERENCES

1. Galatians 6:2
2. 1 John 3:16
3. Proverbs 15:14
4. Sirach 42:18, Hebrew Text
5. Isaiah 58:6-8, 10
6. Testament of Naphtali 2:8
7. Enoch 14:2
8. St. Mark 8:17
9. St. Mark 6:52
10. Ephesians 4:18
11. Romans 10:10
12. St. Mark 16:14
13. Acts 19:9
14. Hebrews 3:12
15. Proverbs 28:5
16. St. Mark 1:15
17. Acts 20:21
18. Isaiah 43:10
19. Odes of Solomon 4:5
20. Odes of Solomon 8:10, 11
21. Isaiah 7:9, Greek, Syriac, and Old Latin Texts
22. Clement of Alexandria, *Exhortation*. Chapter X
23. 2 Corinthians 4:4
24. St. Clement's *1st Epistle to Corinthians* 3:4
25. Psalm 17:15
26. St. John 6:69
27. 2 Timothy 1:12
28. Hebrews 11:6
29. Hebrews 11:1
30. Ephesians 2:8
31. Psalm 111:10
32. St. James 2:23
33. Genesis 15:6
34. Deuteronomy 6:25
35. Psalm 34:14
36. St. James 2:5
37. 2 Corinthians 8:14
38. 1 John 3:2

39. 1 Corinthians 13:12
40. Sirach 2:6
41. Psalm 119:66
42. 3 Enoch 48:10D; Zohar 1:37b
43. 2 Baruch 54:5
44. Sirach 2:10
45. Wisdom 3:9
46. Isaiah 40:26
47. Psalm 19:1
48. Romans 1:20
49. Wisdom 13:5, Latin Vulgate Text
50. Psalm 139:14
51. St. John 5:39
52. Hebrews 11:3
53. Sirach 33:3, Hebrew Text
54. St. John 17:8
55. 1 Corinthians 13:2; St. Matthew 17:20
56. Odes of Solomon 22:7
57. Proverbs 28:5
58. Wisdom 1:1, 2, Latin Vulgate Text

The Reach of Hope

*F*_aith_ gives us the courage we need on our journey towards Him, knowing that "God is our refuge and strength, a ready help in time of trouble, therefore we will not fear."[1] To be without faith is to know fear:

> *When he saw the strong wind, Peter was afraid, and*
> *beginning to sink he cried out, 'Lord, save me.' Jesus*
> *immediately reached out his hand and caught him,*
> *saying to him, 'O man of little faith, why did you doubt?'*[2]

> *Why are you so fearful? Have you no faith?*[3]

> *The fearful and unbelieving*[4]

St. James describes the man of little faith as being double-minded, and a "double-minded man is unstable in all his ways"[5] and just as fearful as a "*double-hearted*"[6] man, the term for a coward in the Old Testament. To have the courage of faith is also to have "the simplicity (*haplotes = singleness*) that is in Christ"[7] : the single-mindedness we need to seek and find the Lord.

Besides faith, we need another helper in our search for the Lord: **hope**. Faith gives us the confident assurance that although we cannot as yet see Him, God is there, waiting for us at the end of our journey. Hope makes us reach out towards Him. Hope keeps us going day after day with the "patience of hope,"[8] and the joy and peace which "lively hope"[9] gives us, if we believe. For we must have faith before we can have hope.

Hope played an important part in the Old Testament, for there are five words in it to describe the various gradations of hope. For a confident hope in God's loving care which included holding fast and entrusting one's cause to Him, the word **betach** is used, often rendered "**trust**." **Chasah**, in turn, conveys the meaning of a **confident hope** in God's help, taking refuge in the Lord, and relying on Him for speedy deliverance. When there was a hope in His goodness with an **expectation of good** from the Lord, and a looking forward to future gladness, **tocheleth** was the word used. And because - to test our endurance - there is often some delay in God's promised help, **patient hope** was expressed by the word **yachal**. Lastly, **kavah** denoted **heroic hope**, the kind of hope that continues hoping despite every misfortune. Saint Paul described one possessing it as he "who against hope believed in hope."[10]

Our Lord admires faith in us: "O woman, great is your faith! Be it done to you according as you will";[11] "He marveled, and said to those who followed Him: 'Truly, I say to you, not even in Israel have I found such great faith.'"[12] But He is moved by our hope in Him, our trust in His goodness:

The Lord takes pleasure... in those who hope for His mercy.[13]

The only instance in the Gospels where our Lord unsolicitedly asked someone if he wanted to be healed, was to the cripple who waited hopefully for thirty-eight years, to be immersed at the right moment into the waters of a miraculous pool.[14] In the Parable of the Laborers in the Vineyard,[15] the last workers were paid first, because they hoped the longest to be hired standing "all day" in the market place up to "the eleventh hour," when they were finally hired. They did not give up and go home, but heroically waited there, hoping in God's providence. We must not forget what the poet Milton said: "They also serve who "stand and wait"[16] - hopefully.

What are the signs of that true hope that moves the heart of God?

True hope does not trust in vanities:

"If I have made gold my hope or called fine gold my confidence, if I had rejoiced because of my wealth's greatness or because I had many possessions... I would have denied that God is above."[17]

True hope does not trust in man alone:

Thus says the Lord: 'Cursed is the man who trusts in man and relies on flesh as his arm and departs from the Lord.'[18]

True hope does not even trust in righteousness:

I say to the righteous... if he trusts in his righteousness and commits iniquity, none of his righteousness will be remembered, but in the iniquity he has committed he shall die.[19]

True hope does not rest in the externals of religion alone:

Do not trust in these deceptive words: This is the Temple of the Lord, the Temple of the Lord, the Temple of the Lord.[20]

True hope relies on God alone and His goodness:

Happy is he... whose hope is in the Lord his God.[21]

Lord, what do I wait for? My hope is in You[22]

As in faith, so also in hope, there is an element of the unseen, for "hope that is seen is not hope. For who hopes in what he sees?"[23] The hope of the Old Testament is in God, who was never seen, but Christian hope is more fortunate because our hope is in God who came down and was made flesh and dwelt in our midst. And who is to come again:

For the grace of God has appeared for the salvation of all men, training us to renounce ungodliness and worldly lusts, and to live sober, upright, and godly lives in this world awaiting our blessed Hope, the appearing of the glory of our great God and Savior: Jesus Christ who gave Himself for us to redeem us.[24]

True Christian hope is a hope full of joy because "the Lord Jesus Christ is our hope,"[25] and if we are good we carry this Living Hope within us:

This Mystery… which is Christ in you, the hope of glory.[26]

We do not walk alone. The great gifts of understanding, faith and hope are given to us to be shared with others along the way. Love shares faith in Him and is always ready to give hope to those in need. The wonderful thing about giving hope to others is that we gain it for ourselves when we need it the most. Let us remember that He "went about doing good and healing all who were oppressed,"[27] but also giving hope by a kind word of encouragement:

Son, take courage, your sins are forgiven.[28]

Daughter, take courage, your faith has made you whole.[29]

Take heart, it is I; do not be afraid.[30]

And so did His disciples when they said to the blind man who cried out to the Lord:

Take heart, rise, He is calling you.[31]

It is a very holy thing to comfort others in their time of grief, to give them hope in a time of darkness, and thereby anchor them to the peace of God. For when we comfort one another we do the work of the Holy Spirit of God: the holy Comforter of our souls. Who knows what might have happened if someone had given hope to the one who betrayed our Lord in the remorseful moment of His greatest need? But instead…

When Judas, His betrayer, saw that He was condemned, he regretted it and brought back the thirty pieces of silver to the chief priests and the elders saying, 'I have sinned in betraying innocent blood.' They said, 'What is that to us? See to it yourself.' And throwing down the pieces of silver in the Temple he departed, and he went and hanged himself.[32]

There were once three sisters. The eldest was most admirable; she was a valiant woman who accomplished everything she made up her mind to do. Courageous and direct, she always knew that what she said was true. She never took the word "*impossible*" for an answer but confidently went ahead wherever she felt called. There was never any hesitation on her part, and she did not tolerate any doubts. Never would she have anything to do with those who scoffed, and she avoided all duplicity. What a splendid woman she was: her name was **Faith**.

There was another sister who was very beautiful indeed, and beloved by all, for she was so gracious and always went about doing good. She never said anything unkind or thought evil of others, for she was very patient and sympathetic towards all who came her way. Everything she did was done with tenderness, because her name was **Love**.

There was yet another sister, the quiet one, not as fascinating as her sister Faith nor so appealing as her sister Love. Nevertheless, there was something about **Hope** that was quite unique in an unobtrusive way, for you see, Hope went where no one else seemed to go - we mean the dark and gloomy corridors where despair is found. Truly, there was something wonderful about the way she would seek out and sit beside the lonely, the sick, the frightened and discouraged, and all those who were desolate and depressed. She loved the desperate, for they needed her the most, and whenever she would hear them sigh she would quickly be by their side caressing their brow and whispering endearments.

O, blessed are those who bring Hope to Despair, for Faith and Love do always come after her.

REFERENCES

1. Psalm 46:1, 2
2. St. Matthew 14:30-31
3. St. Mark 4:40
4. Revelation 21:8; Sirach 2:13
5. St. James 1:8
6. 1 Chronicles 12:33
7. 2 Corinthians 11:3
8. 1 Thessalonians 1:3
9. 1 Peter 1:3
10. Romans 4:18
11. St. Matthew 15:28
12. St. Matthew 8:10; St. Luke 7:9
13. Psalm 147:11
14. St. John 5:2-15
15. St. Matthew 20:1-16
16. John Milton, "On His Blindness" XVI
17. Job 31:24-25, 28
18. Jeremiah 17:5
19. Ezekiel 33:13
20. Jeremiah 7:4
21. Psalm 146:5
22. Psalm 39:7
23. Romans 8:24
24. Titus 2:11-13
25. 1 Timothy 1:1
26. Colossians 1:27
27. Acts 10:38
28. St. Matthew 9:2
29. St. Matthew 9:22; St. Luke 8:48
30. St. Matthew 14:27; St. Mark 6:50
31. St. Mark 10:49
32. St. Matthew 27:3-5

The Touch of Love

W hen we shall begin to love others with the same love that He has for us, and become aware of the goodness of God in others and His loving care for them as well: we shall be mindful of the needs of others, their hopes, their fears, their confusion, their loneliness and despair. And we shall seek them out and bring them His love, as He sought us and found us, and gave us all His love.

When we can forgive and love generously, even utterly at the very time our deeply wounded heart is in need of the balm of its own love... when we can keep our arms outstretched in loving, notwithstanding the numbing cold of a hate that rebuffs... when we are there, all eyes, all ears, all loving aid to every need before it has to cry out, we shall then be loving as we should, and we shall joyfully know that we are drawing near to Him. For it is through love that we come close to God and He comes close to us.

There will be times we shall feel no desire to love, times when there may be someone before us who is unlovable to us – inasmuch as there may be some persons we have no sympathy for, some people alien to our own natural liking, and even some who arouse antipathy in us. It is when we do not feel like loving and yet we nevertheless love in action because of the need for our love, that a wonderful thing shall happen: in that very moment of selfless loving we shall know that God is love in our hearts. For in that instant when we have no other thought than the need of another to be loved by us, a great new love will suddenly surge forth from our hearts, shattering the barrier that kept back the flow of our own human love.

In our search of God, as we help each other along the way, sharing our faith, giving hope, and bearing one another's burdens in love: we shall catch a glimpse of the brightness of His glory towards us, which shall quicken our faith, and make our hope abound.

Faith and hope are perfected in Love. Love is the aim of all the teaching we receive from both the Old and New Testaments. As St. Paul said:

Love is the fulfillment of the Law.[1]

The whole Law is fulfilled in one word... love.[2]

He who loves his neighbor has fulfilled the Law.[3]

Thus, it is important that we should know what love is all about. The Gospels have two words for "**love**": ***phileo*** and ***agape***. There is another word for "love" in Greek: *eros*, but it is never used in the New Testament because of its erotic significations.

Phileo is human love, such as the love of a father for his son, the love of a mother for her daughter, the love between friends and between a man and a woman. It is part of human nature to *phileo*: to love nobly and unselfishly.

Agape or ***agapesis*** is - strictly speaking - supernatural love, the love of God for man, and of man for God and for his friend or neighbor: for the love of God.

Where the New Testament tells us to "make love your aim"[4] and "above all things have fervent love for one another,"[5] the kind of love that is spoken about is not ordinary human "love" (***phileo***) but God's way of loving: ***agape***.

What is it that is so different about agape? The kind of love He commanded us to have for one another:

A new Commandment I give to you, that you love (agape) one another as I have loved (agape) you.[6]

First of all we should know that it is a very special gift from the Lord to us. God Himself places it in our hearts:

We love (agape) Him because He first loved (agape) us.[7]

God's love (agape) has been poured into our hearts by the Holy Spirit who has been given to us.[8]

Secondly, we should know that we have to be good, in order to be able to possess it and love as God does, and as He wills us to love Him and one another:

For this is the Love (agape) of God, that we keep His Commandments.[9]

This is love (agape), that we follow His Commandments.[10]

The Lord Himself said:

He who has my Commandments and keeps them, he it is who loves (agape) Me.[11]

If a man loves (agape) Me, he will keep My word.[12]

If you keep My Commandments you will abide in My love (agape).[13]

To have "love" (agape), we not only have to be good, but we also have to be kind, for:

Love (agape) does no wrong to a neighbor.[14]

If anyone has the world's goods and sees his brother in need, yet closes his heart against him, how does God's love (agape) abide in him?[15]

If we love (agape) one another, God dwells in us, and His love (agape) is perfected in us.[16]

The most important thing about *agape* - the love that only the good and kind can have in their hearts - is that it is a super-natural love, a love literally out of this world, and the most personal thing God can give us. It is the greatest of all His gifts, because it is through love (*agape*) that we can intimately know Him:

Love (agape) is of God, and he who loves (agape) is born of God and knows God.[17]

And this is so "because God is Love (*agape*)."[18] Love is His very Being. That is why "he who does not love (*agape*) does not know God."[19]

The great love of God is made manifest and tangible to us in Jesus, our Lord:

In this the love (agape) of God was made manifest among us, in that God sent His only Son into the world so that we might live through Him.[20]

And it is through the exercise of that same wonderful *agape* that our Lord laid down His life for us:

By this we know love (agape), in that He laid down His life for us.[21]

"Beloved, if God so loved (*agape*) us, so ought we also to love (*agape*) one another"[22] by doing the same thing He did for us: "lay down our lives for"[23] each other.

And that is where we have the basic difference between the three forms of love. With *eros* our love is *possessive - selfish*; with *phileo* our love is *generous - unselfish*; with *agape* our love can be *heroic - selfless*:

He that loses his life for My sake will find it.[24]

I saw the souls of those who had been beheaded for their testimony to Jesus and for the Word of God.[25]

They loved (agape) not their lives even unto death. [26]

That element of selfless loving is what makes our Lord's Commandment in the Gospels "new." For in the Old Testament we were commanded to love our neighbor as ourself:

You shall love your neighbor as yourself.[27]

Hence, when the repentant people asked St. John the Baptist - the greatest prophet of the Old Testament - what they were to do to amend their lives, he said to them:

He who has two coats, let him share with him who has none, and he who has food let him do likewise.[28]

In other words, if any one of them had two coats, he was to give one to a needy person but keep the other for himself, and if he had two loaves of bread, he was to give one to the hungry, but keep the other to provide for himself in fulfillment of the injunction to love one's self also.

Our Lord's new Commandment demands something more than that of us:

A new Commandment I give unto you, that you love (agape) one another as I have loved (agape) you.[29]

Greater love (agape) has no man than this, that a man lay down his life for his friends.[30]

I lay down My life.[31]

We are now commanded to love our neighbor *more* than ourself, even to the laying down of our life for him, because we no longer consider him a neighbor but a friend.

No longer are we to hold back our portion or take into

consideration our own needs, but rather we are to love to the total giving up of self, and of what belongs to self. This is what *agape* is all about:

> *From him who takes away your cloak do not withhold your coat as well.*[32]

> *If any one forces you to go one mile, go with him two miles.*[33]

Moreover, we are commanded to do something which is humanly impossible to do unless we have supernatural love within us:

> *Love (agape) your enemies, bless them that curse you, do good to them that hate you, and pray for them who persecute you.*[34]

The unerring sign that God's *agape* abides in us is our ability to love those who are hurting us, and to do good towards them.

It is in the act of selfless loving: of laying down our lives for others, and giving up our wants to fill their needs - that we shall experience the love of the Father in our hearts, just as the Son felt it who lived and died for us:

> *Therefore does My Father love Me because I lay down My life.*[35]

The Lord, who told us to follow Him, gave us the good example of first doing Himself what He asked us to accomplish. For when He commanded us to love one another, even to the giving up of our lives, He laid down a command that He was also commanded to do and did for our sakes:

> *I lay down My life... this Commandment have I received from My Father.*[36]

> *He laid down His life for us.*[37]

And He prayed for us to the Father: "that the love with which

You have loved Me may be in them and I in them."**38**

How wisely He prayed indeed, because we shall need Him within us to show us how to exercise that great love which belongs to God alone, for we poor children do not know how to administer it. Do we not remember St. Peter's reckless boast and our Lord's reply?

> 'Lord... I will lay down my life for You.' And Jesus answered him, 'Will you lay down your life for My sake? Truly, truly, I say to you, the cock will not crow, till you have denied Me three times.'**39**

And so, when God places His love in our hearts, He does a wonderful thing: He gives it to us in Jesus, whom He sows in our hearts as a Seed. For the Son is the Word of God: "the implanted Word which is able to save your souls"**40** - "the Seed of God which abides in"**41** us if we believe in Him. Did you know that within you is "the inner man... Christ dwelling in your hearts through faith"**42** "the hidden man of the heart"?**43** God's love is within us in our Lord Jesus Christ as a Seed to be increased in our hearts in proportion to our giving up of self to Him, just as the ground gives of itself to make all seeds increase and bear fruit:

> He must increase and I must decrease.**44**

> Herein is My Father glorified in that you bear much fruit.**45**

> He who abides in Me and I in him, he it is who bears much fruit, for without Me you can do nothing.**46**

We learn to love as our Lord loves by giving up ourself, by emptying ourselves for Him as "Jesus... emptied Himself" **47** for us. We do that every time we selflessly love one another in loving kindness and compassion.

And as He thereby increases in us, we conform ourselves to Him so that we may "grow up in every way unto Him."**48** This we accomplish through our fidelity to His Word, for to love is also to keep His Commandments. Thus through fidelity and loving kindness His love is perfected in us:

Whoever keeps His Word - in him truly is the love of God perfected.[49]

If we love one another, God dwells in us, and His love is perfected in us.[50]

God's love is not only placed in our hearts as a Seed, but also upon us as an oversized garment which we are to fill up as He increases in us. We keep in our hearts the love of God in Jesus, and we also "put on Christ":[51]

Put on the Lord Jesus Christ.[52]

Put on the new man created after the likeness of God in true righteousness and holiness.[53]

No one shall put on the likeness of God unless he has first put off the old man with all his lusts and evil desires:

Put off the old man.[54]

Put to death what is earthly in us: immorality, impurity, passion, evil desire and covetousness, which is idolatry.[55]

Put off all... anger, wrath, malice, slander, and foul talk.[56]

And in their stead:

Put on then, as God's chosen ones, holy and beloved, compassion, kindness, lowliness, meekness, and patience, forbearing one another and, if one has a complaint against another, forgiving each other; as the Lord has forgiven you, so you also most forgive. And above all these put on love, which binds everything together in perfect harmony.[57]

To really love as we should takes good effort on our part, and patience:

> *Make every effort to supplement your faith with virtue, and virtue with knowledge, and knowledge with self-control, and self-control with steadfastness, and steadfastness with godliness, and godliness with brotherly affection, and brotherly affection with love.*[58]

The love (*agape*) of God is holy and we must be purified before we can love one another fervently and wholeheartedly, for:

> *Love (agape)... issues from a pure heart and a good conscience and sincere faith.*[59]

> *Having purified your souls by your obedience to the truth for a sincere brotherly affection, love one another from the heart intensely.*[60]

When we want to know whether or not we have the love of God in our hearts, we recall the signs of His love in us:

> *Love is patient and kind... not jealous or boastful; it is not arrogant or rude. Love does not insist on its own way; it is not easily provoked, thinks no evil, rejoices not in iniquity but rejoices in the Truth. Love bears all things, believes all things, hopes all things, endures all things. Love never fails.*[61]

Let us not take the love of God for granted, but keep diligent watch to preserve it as we have received it from the Lord, because love can grow cold. There are two things which make the love of God grow cold in our hearts: the sensory allurements of evil "lusts and pleasures,"[62] and a surfeit of worldly possessions:

> *Because iniquity will abound, the love (agape) of many will grow cold.*[63]

*You are neither hot nor cold.... You are lukewarm because you
say, 'I am rich, I have prospered, I need nothing.'* **64**

What both of these have in common is that they rob us of
that thing which the Lord wants the most from us: desire for
Him. Since we are human, the lures of iniquity attract our desire,
and as for those who have everything and want nothing, how can
they have desire in their hearts?

In our love for Him, let us not underestimate the power of
desire, for it is in our longing and desire for Him that human
and divine love shall embrace.

Never forget that the Lord desires towards Him: the fierce
possessiveness of our own *eros*, and the warmth of our human
love, for with these arms of our own loving shall we cling to Him
and never let Him go:

Cleave unto the Lord your God. **65**

*Love the Lord your God. Oh... that you would cling to Him, for
He is your life and the length of your days.* **66**

Love the Lord your God... with all your strength. **67**

Let us long for Him, sigh for Him, and yearn for the Lord
our God.

Let us pine for Him, languish for Him and seek Him with all
the desire of our hearts - and we shall quickly find Him by our
side.

For the Lord is drawn to us by our desire for Him - drawn by
that special touch of our human love.

When was the last time we desired Him?

When was the last time we hungered for God?

REFERENCES

1. Romans 13:10
2. Galatians 5:14
3. Romans 13:8
4. 1 Corinthians 14:1
5. 1 Peter 4:8
6. St. John 13:34
7. 1 John 4:19
8. Romans 5:5
9. 1 John 5:3
10. 2 John v. 6
11. St. John 14:21
12. St. John 14:23
13. St. John 15:10
14. Romans 13:10
15. 1 John 3:17
16. 1 John 4:12
17. 1 John 4:7
18. 1 John 4:8, 16
19. 1 John 4:8
20. 1 John 4:9
21. 1 John 3:16
22. 1 John 4:11
23. 1 John 3:16
24. St. Matthew 10:39; St. Mark 8:35
25. Revelation 20:4
26. Revelation 12:11
27. Leviticus 19:18
28. St. Luke 3:11
29. St. John 13:34
30. St. John 15:13
31. St. John 10:15, 17
32. St. Luke 6:29; St. Matthew 5:40
33. St. Matthew 5:41
34. St. Matthew 5:44
35. St. John 10:17
36. St. John 10:17, 18
37. 1 John 3:16
38. St. John 17:26

39. St. John 13:37, 38
40. St. James 1:21
41. 1 John 3:9
42. Ephesians 3:16, 17
43. 1 Peter 3:4
44. St. John 3:30
45. St. John 15:8
46. St. John 15:5
47. Philippians 2:7
48. Ephesians 4:15
49. 1 John 2:5
50. 1 John 4:12
51. Galatians 3:27
52. Romans 13:14
53. Ephesians 4:24
54. Ephesians 4:22
55. Colossians 3:5
56. Colossians 3:8
57. Colossians 3:12-14
58. 2 Peter 1:5-7
59. 1 Timothy 1:5
60. 1 Peter 1:22
61. 1 Corinthians 13:4-8
62. Titus 3:3
63. St. Matthew 24:12
64. Revelation 3:15, 16, 17
65. Joshua 23:8
66. Deuteronomy 30:20
67. Deuteronomy 6:5